LOOKING INTO THE

ATMOSPHERE

BY MARTHA LONDON

The Child's World®
childsworld.com

Published by The Child's World®
1980 Lookout Drive • Mankato, MN 56003-1705
800-599-READ • www.childsworld.com

ISBN 9781503835160
LCCN 2019943111

Printed in the United States of America

ABOUT THE AUTHOR
Martha London writes books for young readers full-time. When she isn't writing, you can find her hiking in the woods.

TABLE OF CONTENTS

CHAPTER ONE

The Atmosphere's Layers . . . 4

CHAPTER TWO

The Troposphere . . . 7

CHAPTER THREE

The Stratosphere . . . 10

CHAPTER FOUR

The Mesosphere . . . 15

CHAPTER FIVE

The Thermosphere and Beyond . . . 19

Fast Facts . . . 21

Glossary . . . 22

To Learn More . . . 23

Index . . . 24

The Atmosphere's Layers

Earth is surrounded by a ball of air called the atmosphere. The atmosphere extends to the edge of outer space. Scientists have divided Earth's atmosphere into five layers. The lowest layers are the troposphere and the stratosphere. They reach just a few miles above Earth's surface. In the middle is the mesosphere. The highest layers are the thermosphere and exosphere. They stretch hundreds to thousands of miles up.

Each layer has different features. One supports life. Another protects Earth from harmful sunrays. Some layers have weather. And one is home to **satellites** that send and receive messages from Earth.

Layers of the Atmosphere

Exosphere
370–6,200 mi (600–10,000 km)

Thermosphere
53–370 mi (85–600 km)

Spacecraft

Satellites

Mesosphere
31–53 mi (50–85 km)

Aurora

Stratosphere
11–31 mi (18–50 km)

Ozone Layer

Meteors

Troposphere
0–11 mi (0–18 km)

Airplanes

Birds fly in the troposphere.

CHAPTER TWO

The Troposphere

The troposphere is the layer closest to Earth's surface. It is the first layer of the atmosphere. The troposphere is one of the thinnest layers. It extends from the surface up to 11 miles (18 km) high.

The troposphere contains about 80 percent of Earth's atmosphere. It has more air **molecules** than the higher layers. People and animals breathe the air. The air needs to be about one-quarter oxygen for people and animals to live. The troposphere is the only layer where there is enough oxygen. The troposphere is **dense**. It is thickest at Earth's surface. The air molecules are pushed together by the weight of the atmosphere above.

Temperatures vary in the troposphere. The troposphere is warmest at Earth's surface. The thicker air holds more heat. The surface can reach temperatures of 130 degrees Fahrenheit (54°C). As **altitude** increases, the air gets thinner. Thin air does not hold as much heat.

The air is cold at mountaintops because they are at high altitudes.

Ninety-nine percent of the atmosphere's moisture is in the troposphere.

High altitude is one reason why some mountaintops have snow even in the summer. At the outer edge of the troposphere, the temperature drops to 112 degrees below zero (–80°C).

Weather occurs in the troposphere. Weather is caused by the movement of air. The air's movement creates wind. Wind pushes the clouds. Clouds form when air cools and lets go of moisture. Warm, moist air is unstable. Very unstable air creates storms.

CHAPTER THREE

The Stratosphere

The stratosphere starts where the troposphere ends. It extends 31 miles (50 km) above Earth's surface. The stratosphere is home to the ozone layer. Ozone is a type of gas made of oxygen. The ozone layer absorbs **ultraviolet (UV) radiation**. UV radiation comes from the sun. It is harmful to people. It causes sunburns and skin cancer. The ozone layer blocks most UV radiation. This keeps the radiation away from Earth's surface.

Unlike the troposphere, the stratosphere gets warmer higher up. The ozone layer holds heat from the sun's rays. This causes the temperature in the stratosphere to rise. At the top of the layer, air temperatures reach 32 degrees Fahrenheit (0°C).

If there were no ozone, the sun would make life on Earth impossible.

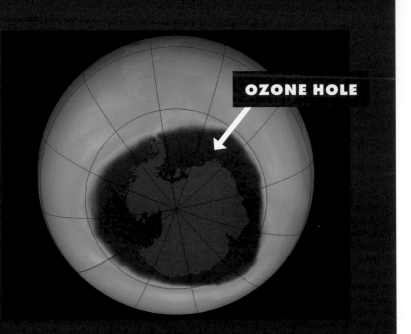

OZONE HOLE

Repairing the Ozone

Over many years, the ozone layer thinned. This let in more UV rays. People were polluting the air with certain chemicals. The chemicals hurt the ozone layer. But people stopped using those chemicals. Now the ozone layer is repairing itself. It will take many years before it will completely repair.

Scientists fly weather balloons into the stratosphere. The weather balloons collect information about the atmosphere. They measure air quality, wind, and temperature. These measurements help scientists predict the weather.

The air in the stratosphere is more stable than air in the troposphere. Some planes fly in the lower part of the stratosphere. This helps them avoid bumpy air. They can also avoid flying through bad weather. But planes and weather balloons cannot reach the top of the stratosphere. The air is 1,000 times thinner there than it is at Earth's surface.

Thin air cannot hold up planes. Weather balloons pop high up in the stratosphere. The air inside them expands as they rise. They pop when the air expands too much.

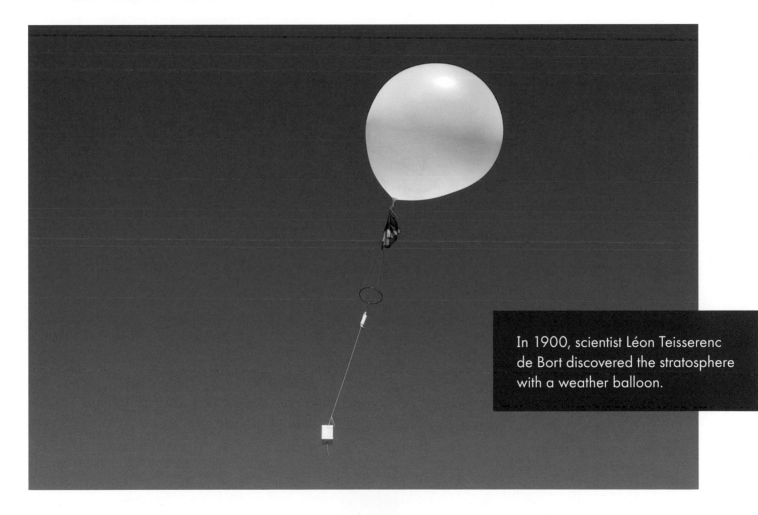

In 1900, scientist Léon Teisserenc de Bort discovered the stratosphere with a weather balloon.

Meteors are also known
as shooting stars.

CHAPTER FOUR

The Mesosphere

The mesosphere is the third layer of the atmosphere. It extends 53 miles (85 km) above Earth's surface. Air is too thin to breathe in the mesosphere. In this layer, the air cools again. The mesosphere has very little ozone in it. It cannot hold heat as well as the stratosphere can. Its temperatures can drop as low as –130 degrees Fahrenheit (–90°C).

The mesosphere protects Earth from **meteors**. Meteors enter the atmosphere. But most do not reach Earth's surface. They burn up in the mesosphere. Meteors travel at thousands of miles per hour. When one hits the atmosphere, the temperature around it rises. The meteor burns at 3,000 degrees Fahrenheit (1,650°C).

Meteors burn up. But they do not disappear. Tiny parts of the meteors stay in the mesosphere. The air in the mesosphere contains **particles** of iron and other metals. There are more metal particles in the mesosphere than in other layers. These particles come from the metals in meteors.

It is hard to study the mesosphere. Weather balloons and planes cannot reach it. Satellites circle Earth too high. So scientists launch rockets. The rockets measure temperatures and air movement in the mesosphere. But the rockets cannot stay in this layer. They fall back to the ground. Scientists get most of their information on the mesosphere from these brief measurements.

The rockets scientists use to study the atmosphere are called sounding rockets.

Auroras near the North Pole are called aurora borealis (uh-ROR-uh bor-ee-AL-iss).

CHAPTER FIVE

The Thermosphere and Beyond

The thermosphere is the fourth layer. This layer extends up to 370 miles (600 km) above Earth's surface. The thermosphere's temperatures can reach more than 3,000 degrees Fahrenheit (2,000°C). Oxygen molecules in the thermosphere absorb the sun's light. The sun heats each molecule more because there are fewer of them. But the molecules are so far apart that people would not be able to feel the heat.

Solar storms occur in the thermosphere. Solar storms happen when bursts of particles from the sun travel through space. The particles from the sun strike particles in Earth's atmosphere. They release energy in the form of colored light. The colors seem to wave in the sky. These colorful storms are called auroras.

Satellites circle Earth in the thermosphere. The International Space Station (ISS) is a satellite. Astronauts live in the ISS. There are almost 2,000 active satellites circling Earth.

Above the thermosphere is the exosphere. The exosphere extends from the edge of the thermosphere up to 6,200 miles (10,000 km) above Earth's surface. The exosphere is the limit of Earth's atmosphere. Air is very thin in the exosphere. The outer edge of the exosphere is hard to detect.

Scientists are still learning about Earth's atmosphere. But they know that each layer is important for the health of the planet. The layers of the atmosphere protect Earth. They make life possible.

FAST FACTS

- Earth's atmosphere has five layers: troposphere, stratosphere, mesosphere, thermosphere, and exosphere.

- The troposphere is closest to Earth's surface.

- Most weather happens in the troposphere.

- The stratosphere gets warmer with increased altitude.

- The ozone layer is in the stratosphere. It protects Earth from UV radiation.

- The mesosphere is hard for scientists to study.

- Meteors burn up in the mesosphere.

- The thermosphere is where satellites circle Earth.

- The exosphere is the outer limit of Earth's atmosphere.

altitude (AL-ti-tood) Altitude is the height above the ground. Air is thinner at a higher altitude.

dense (DENSS) Dense means heavy or packed together. Air in the troposphere is dense.

meteors (MEE-tee-urz) Meteors are pieces of space rock that enter the atmosphere. Meteors burn up.

molecules (MOL-uh-kyoolz) Molecules are the smallest parts of a substance. Molecules in the thermosphere are far apart.

particles (PAR-tuh-kulz) Particles are very small pieces of something. The mesosphere contains iron particles.

satellites (SAT-uh-lites) Satellites are spacecraft that circle a planet. Satellites circle Earth in the thermosphere.

ultraviolet (UV) radiation (uhl-truh-VY-uh-lit ray-dee-AY-shun) Ultraviolet (UV) radiation is harmful rays of light that come from the sun. The ozone layer blocks most ultraviolet (UV) radiation.

TO LEARN MORE

IN THE LIBRARY

Borngraber, Elizabeth. *The Layers of Earth's Atmosphere*. New York, NY: PowerKids Press, 2018.

Greek, Joe. *What Is the Atmosphere?* New York, NY: Britannica Educational Publishing, 2015.

Slingerland, Janet. *What Makes the Sky Blue?* Mankato, MN: The Child's World, 2017.

ON THE WEB

Visit our website for links about the atmosphere:

childsworld.com/links

Note to Parents, Teachers, and Librarians: We routinely verify our Web links to make sure they are safe and active sites. So encourage your readers to check them out!

altitude, 8-9, 21

auroras, 5, 19

exosphere, 4, 5, 20, 21

mesosphere, 4, 5, 15-16, 21

meteors, 5, 15-16, 21

molecules, 7, 19

oxygen, 7, 10, 19

ozone, 5, 10, 12, 15, 21

planes, 5, 12-13, 16

rockets, 16

satellites, 4, 5, 16, 20, 21

solar storms, 19

stratosphere, 4, 5, 10-13, 15, 21

thermosphere, 4, 5, 19-20, 21

troposphere, 4, 5, 7-9, 10, 12, 21

ultraviolet (UV) radiation, 10, 12, 21

weather, 4, 9, 12, 21

weather balloons, 12-13, 16